Deadly Snakes

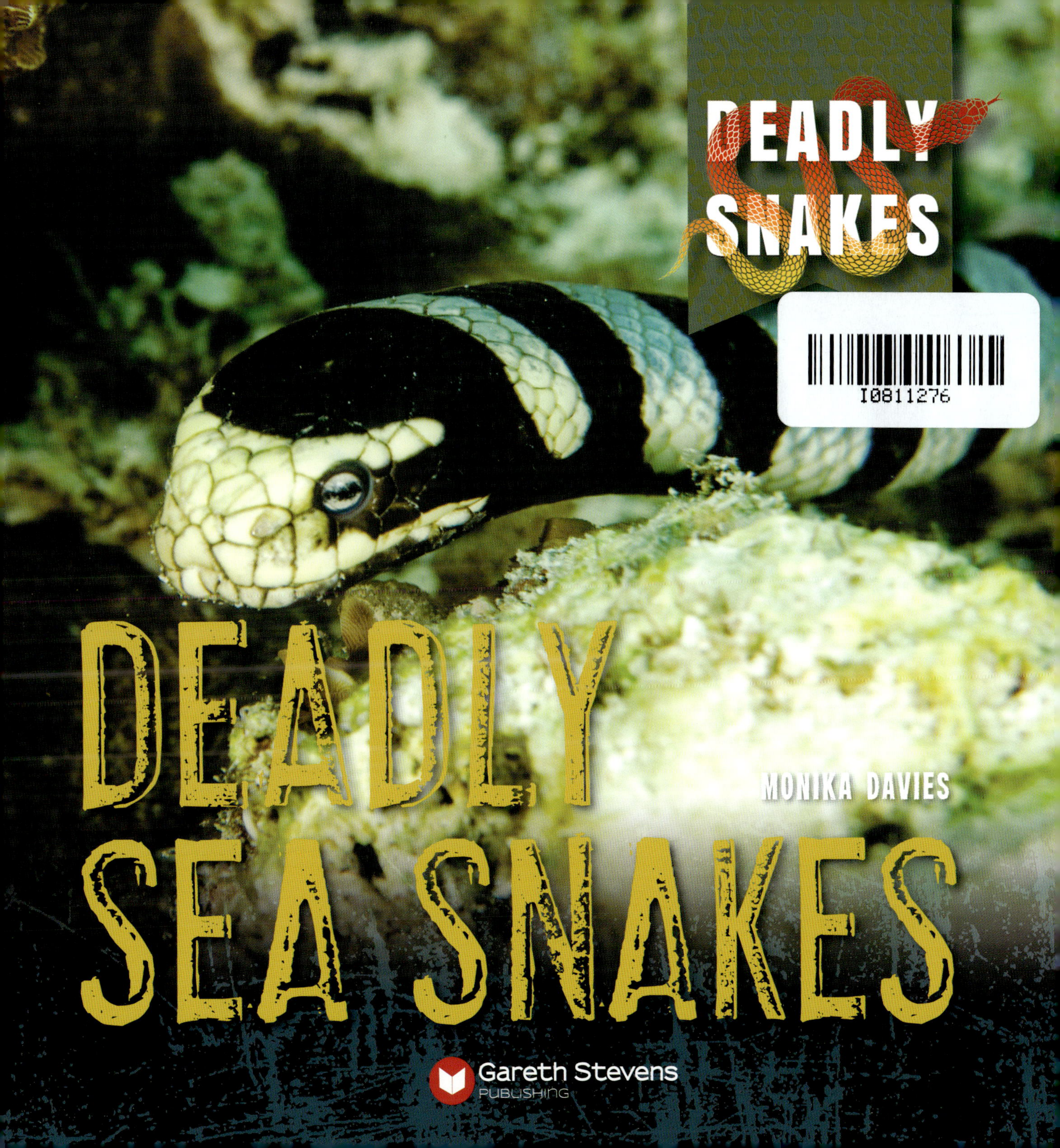

Deadly Sea Snakes

Monika Davies

Gareth Stevens Publishing

Please visit our website, www.garethstevens.com. For a free color catalog of all our high-quality books, call toll free 1-800-542-2595 or fax 1-877-542-2596.

Library of Congress Cataloging-in-Publication Data
Names: Davies, Monika, author.
Title: Deadly sea snakes / Monika Davies.
Description: New York : Gareth Stevens Publishing, [2023] | Series: Deadly snakes | Includes index.
Identifiers: LCCN 2021050749 (print) | LCCN 2021050750 (ebook) | ISBN 9781538279885 (set) | ISBN 9781538279892 (library binding) | ISBN 9781538279878 (paperback) | ISBN 9781538279908 (ebook)
Subjects: LCSH: Sea snakes–Juvenile literature. | Poisonous snakes–Juvenile literature.
Classification: LCC QL666.O64 D385 2023 (print) | LCC QL666.O64 (ebook) | DDC 597.96/5–dc23/eng/20211201
LC record available at https://lccn.loc.gov/2021050749
LC ebook record available at https://lccn.loc.gov/2021050750

First Edition

Portions of this work were originally authored by Gale George and published as *Sea Snakes.* All new material in this edition authored by Monika Davies.

Published in 2023 by
Gareth Stevens Publishing
29 E. 21st Street
New York, NY 10010

Designer: Sheryl Kober
Editor: Monika Davies

Photo credits: Cover, p. 1 fenkieandreas/Shutterstock.com; cover (snake illustration) vinap/Shutterstock.com; cover, pp. 1–24 (background texture) Anna Timoshenko/Shutterstock.com; pp. 1–24 (snakeskin) Natalliya85/Shutterstock.com; pp. 1–24 (halftone texture) MPFphotography/Shutterstock.com; pp. 3, 12, 19 (snake illustration) vinap/Shutterstock.com; pp. 4, 7, 8, 15, 20 (fatal facts texture) Pakhnyushchy/Shutterstock.com; pp. 5, 6, 16 Rich Carey/Shutterstock.com, p. 5 (inset) Ethan Daniels /Shutterstock.com; p. 9 YT. Christina/Shutterstock.com; p. 10 Pyty/Shutterstock.com; p. 11 Ken Griffiths/Shutterstock.com; p. 13 Oksana Golubeva/ Shutterstock.com; p. 14 Sahara Frost/Shutterstock.com; p. 17 SaltedLife/Shutterstock.com; p. 18 NickEvansKZN/Shutterstock.com; p. 21 Nur Cresna/Shutterstock.com.

Printed in the United States of America

CPSIA compliance information: Batch #CSGS23: For further information contact Gareth Stevens, New York, New York, at 1-800-542-2595.

CONTENTS

Words in the glossary appear in **bold** type the first time they are used in the text.

SCARY SEA SNAKES

In warm waters, a snake slowly sneaks through a **coral reef**. Nearby, an eel bobs up and down, unaware of the danger nearby. Snap! The snake sinks its fangs—or long, pointed teeth—into the eel, forcing **venom** into the fish. With a quick gulp, the snake swallows its eel meal whole!

Meet the sea snake, the only snake you'll find spending much of its life underwater. While most snakes are skilled swimmers, only sea snakes like their underwater home best.

FATAL FACTS

There are more than 60 different species, or kinds, of sea snakes. The different species of sea snakes fall into two groups: true sea snakes and sea kraits. They are part of the cobra family.

True sea snakes spend nearly their whole life in the water, while sea kraits live on land and in water.

sea krait

Sea snakes usually live and hunt alone, but they come together to mate. Sometimes they're spotted living as a group.

SPY THE SEA SNAKE

Sea snakes can be hard to spot. Sometimes people see a sea snake and think it's an eel. Most eels can breathe underwater, but sea snakes have **lungs** and must surface for air.

Sea snakes are usually 3 to 5 feet (0.9 to 1.5 m) long, but some can grow to nearly 9 feet (2.7 m)! Over time, they've **adapted** to a life in the water. Their tail is flat like a paddle, which helps them swim. The openings of their nose can seal shut to keep water out.

FATAL FACTS

A sea snake's flattened body helps it move quickly through the water. Yellow-bellied sea snakes can dive at speeds faster than 3.3 feet (1 m) per second when they're hunting or need to swim away.

GIVING BIRTH

True sea snakes give birth to live young. They don't lay eggs. Instead, eggs grow and hatch—or break open—inside the mother's body. Mothers usually give birth to about two live young. The size of babies depends on the species. Yellow-bellied sea snakes are born about 10 inches (25.4 cm) long.

Sea kraits leave the water to find a mate and lay their eggs on the shore. They spend time both on land and in water, making them amphibious. Sea kraits also **digest** their food on land.

FATAL FACTS

A sea snake usually sheds its skin every 26 weeks. This helps the snake remove any harmful sea creatures that may be living on its skin, like algae or barnacles.

In the water, true sea snakes sometimes give birth to up to 34 live young!

WHERE YELLOW-BELLIED SEA SNAKES LIVE

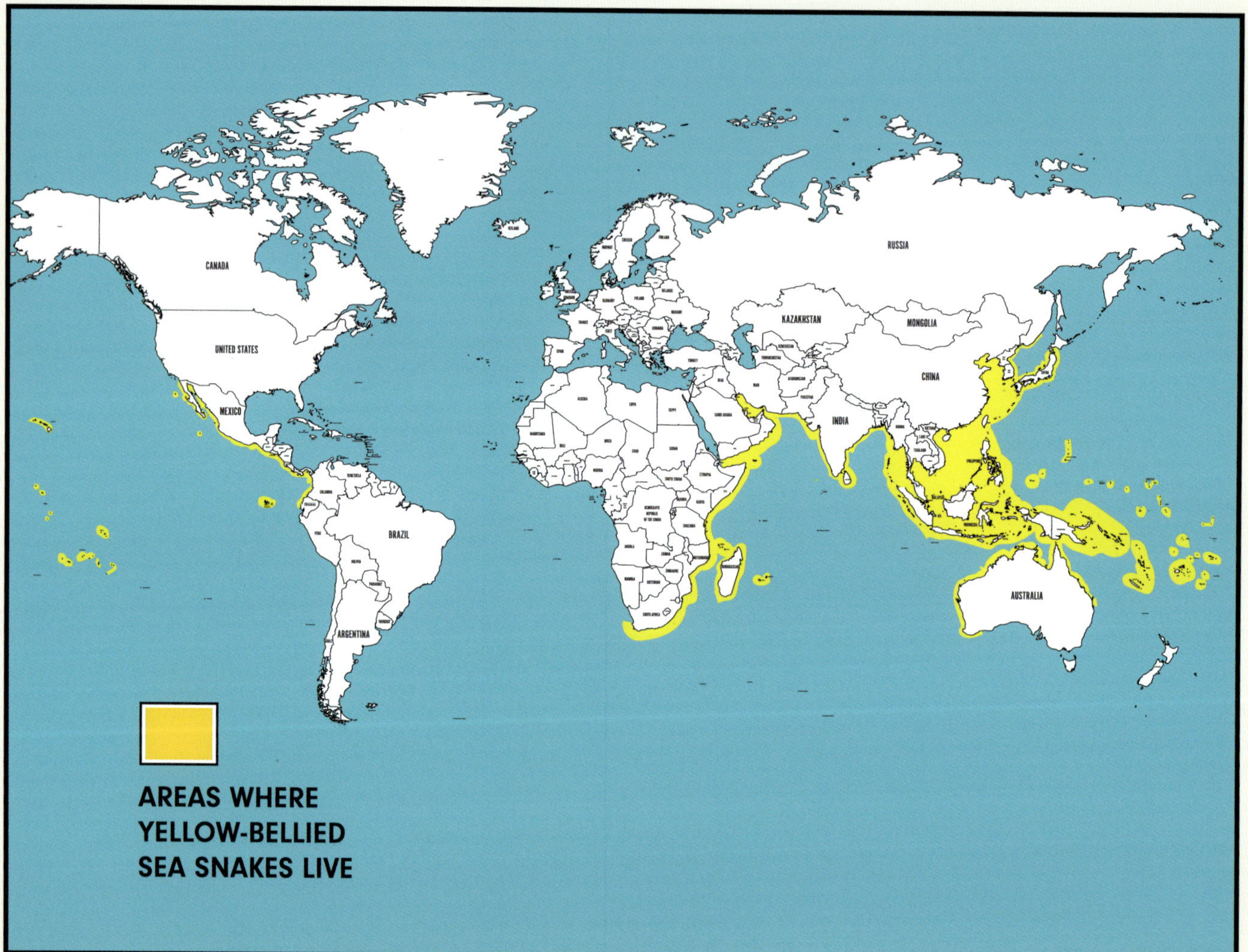

Yellow-bellied sea snakes have even drifted up near California. Unfortunately, these waters are too cold for sea snakes, and they usually cannot survive.

WATERY HABITAT

Sea snakes are named after their watery **habitats.** They mostly live in the warm waters of the Pacific Ocean and Indian Ocean. They live in coral reefs, the open ocean, and other watery places. About half of all sea snake species are found around Australia.

The yellow-bellied sea snake has the largest range of all snake species. They can be found from the eastern coast of Africa to Australia. Ocean currents can carry them as far as The western shores of Central America.

UNDERWATER SENSES

Can sea snakes smell underwater? Yes, they can! Like other snakes, sea snakes can flick out their tongue to "smell" their surroundings. Their tongue passes the smells to the Jacobson's **organ**, which recognizes them. This is how sea snakes investigate, or learn about, their surroundings.

Most sea snakes can also breathe through their skin. This means they can stay underwater longer. True sea snakes have long lungs that help them store air. Sea snakes can dive 800 feet (243.8 m) into the ocean and stay underwater for many hours.

Some sea snakes can swim underwater and not surface for air for up to eight hours—or more!

A recent study showed that olive sea snakes can sense when light falls on their tail. They then tuck their tail away to stay hidden from predators!

SHARP DEFENSES

Sea snakes stay safe by using their **defenses**. These snakes are known for their venomous bite. Their venom is the deadliest out of all venomous snakes! Other sea creatures steer clear of these toxic snakes.

Sea snakes have short, pointed teeth they use for hunting **prey**. They won't usually attack other creatures unless they're bothered by predators, such as sharks and large birds. Some sea snakes are brightly colored, which warns predators to stay away.

FATAL FACTS

Sea snakes may use their flattened tails to trick predators into thinking that they have two heads. Predators might attack the snake's tail, which keeps its head safe.

WHAT'S ON THE MENU?

Different species of sea snakes all have their own favorite meals. Most sea snakes love to eat fish, eels, and crabs. Sea snakes will often eat a huge number of small fish, but they'll also hunt larger fish. Some species only eat fish eggs.

Like other types of snakes, sea snakes can open their jaws wide so they can eat bigger prey. Jaws are the walls of the mouth. While sea snakes are deadly predators, they aren't **aggressive** toward humans and rarely bite people.

Most snakes, including sea snakes, swallow their prey whole. Gulp!

Yellow-bellied sea snakes will drink fresh rainwater that pools on the surface of the ocean. This helps them rehydrate, or obtain a healthy amount of water, after months of no water.

SKILLED HUNTERS

When hunting, sea snakes search around in coral and rocks for prey. They feel vibrations, or small movements, in the water when a fish swims near. That helps them hunt in the dark. Then it's time to strike!

Sea snakes may have short fangs, but their venom is very toxic and works quickly to **paralyze** prey. They mostly use their venom for hunting, not for defense. Venom also helps sea snakes digest their food by breaking down their prey's flesh before they even eat it.

CARING FOR SEA SNAKES

Sea snakes sometimes surprise scuba divers and people who are fishing, but these non-aggressive snakes aren't out to hurt humans. Sea snakes are usually content to keep to themselves.

However, some sea snake species are in danger of dying out. Scientists think this may be due to their ocean habitats getting warmer. Warmer waters harm the health of coral reefs. Losing coral reefs leads to a loss of home and prey for sea snakes.

FATAL FACTS

Sea snakes sometimes approach people because they think people are other sea snakes. Most bites happen when people who are fishing catch surprised sea snakes in their nets.

Climate change, or the changes in Earth's climate due to human activity, are causing the oceans to warm and harming the coral reef habitats sea snakes call home.

GLOSSARY

adapt: to change to suit conditions

aggressive: showing a readiness to attack

coral reef: an underwater hill made up of the hard parts of tiny sea animals

defense: a way of guarding against an enemy

digest: to break down food inside the body so that the body can use it

habitat: the natural place where an animal or plant lives

lung: a part of an animal that takes in air when it breathes

mate: one of two animals that come together to produce babies. Also to come together to make babies.

organ: a part inside an animal's body

paralyze: to make unable to move

prey: an animal that is hunted by other animals for food

venom: something an animal makes in its body that can harm other animals. Venomous means able to produce venom.

FOR MORE INFORMATION

Books

Terp, Gail. *Sea Snakes.* Mankato, MN: Black Rabbit Books, 2021.

Wilson, Sierra. *Sea Snakes.* New York, NY: AV2, 2021.

Websites

Sea Snake

kids.britannica.com/kids/article/sea-snake/353753

Find out more about sea snakes on this website.

Sea Snakes

seaworld.org/animals/facts/reptiles/sea-snakes/

Discover more fun facts about sea snakes here.

Publisher's note to educators and parents: Our editors have carefully reviewed these websites to ensure that they are suitable for students. Many websites change frequently, however, and we cannot guarantee that a site's future contents will continue to meet our high standards of quality and educational value. Be advised that students should be closely supervised whenever they access the internet.

INDEX